WHAT OTHERS ARE SAYING

I think the Homeless Project is a good idea and would be very helpful. I think that if this idea is thought out very carefully, where it is not abused like other systems used for aid, it would be a great help to those who need and want it.

—Robert Demetris
Songwriter/Producer
Esteria Productions

The need for our society to take responsibility for its individuals continues to grow equally as much as the need for us, as individuals, to take responsibility for the betterment of our society as a whole. We may need to determine whether "survival of the fittest" indeed refers to individuals, or to communities, or to nations. Should we continue to drive our homeless from one community to the next, or from one nation to the next?

The very definition of *civilization* includes the words "to have reached a high social development" in many dictionaries. Any project that would not only give our homeless a chance to enjoy the benefits of our society but also give them a chance to *contribute to* the benefits of the same society is a project that helps our nation, or any nation, to reach that higher social development. Our homeless people reflect the greatest flaw in our civilization, and they also present to us the greatest opportunity for us to prove ourselves as a "civilized society."

With all our vacant houses and apartments, with all our discarded clothing and other commodities, and with all our food being thrown out and wasted, we, as a society, simply cannot justify our homeless situation. We need to act now! We need to act as individuals, as communities, and as nations. We have become a "throw-away society" that has been throwing away our most valuable resource—people.

—Terry L. Brooks
Big Brothers of Boone County
Boone County Democratic Committee

This project is of immense opportunity for any community to open their doors to accept their failures and admit the mistakes they have created. And, from our democratic ideals, the opportunity for justice comes from the hope that we can correct that which we have admitted is wrong. The plot thickens as now we must find, within our democratic ways, a clue to be just in dealing with those different in political, economic, and social ways of life.

For whom does responsibility for decent housing rest; the individual family, the housing industry, the national or state governments? Decent housing is a basic necessity for the public welfare. A community offers its best to its least likely citizens. We must refuse to exclude or reject anything that might open the doors to those who have been shunned or pushed away.

I see the beginnings of a greater society as we exchange thoughts to create a task force of community involvement. The task force must be of rotating and lottery forms of engagement. For all to participate and enjoy the leadership drug (power), we must assume responsibility of addressing the majority with the availability of a quality of life we assume exists. Community-wide effort must be a chain of continuous involvement.

—EdD Joslin
Certified Toastmaster

~~THE~~ *Our* HOMELESS DESERVES BETTER

~~THE~~ *Our* HOMELESS DESERVES BETTER

A PLEA TO ALL CARING COMMUNITIES,
BECAUSE ALL HOMELESS PERSONS
ARE SOMEBODY'S RELATIVE

Food
Water

Shelter
Clothies

LA VERNE HUGHES

TATE PUBLISHING
AND ENTERPRISES, LLC

Published by Tate Publishing & Enterprises, LLC
127 E. Trade Center Terrace | Mustang, Oklahoma 73064 USA
1.888.361.9473 | www.tatepublishing.com

Tate Publishing is committed to excellence in the publishing industry. The company reflects the philosophy established by the founders, based on Psalm 68:11,
"The Lord gave the word and great was the company of those who published it."

Book design copyright © 2016 by Tate Publishing, LLC. All rights reserved.
Cover design by Samson Lim
Interior design by Jomar Ouano

Published in the United States of America

ISBN: 978-1-68237-326-2
Social Science / Poverty & Homelessness
15.10.26

Contents

Preface

Strictly from the Heart

This manual is my way of expressing how very, very sorry I am for having had to pass up those homeless persons on street corners. Yes, I passed them by, but my heart always lingered with them. I always wished I could help in some way, but I knew that I was in no position to help them. Not the way that they needed help.

Well, here it is. The way that homeless persons need help is through a *community-wide* effort. So it's not just for me to do something, it's not just for you to do something, but it's for the whole community to come together and do something.

This manual outlines how *any* community can help their homeless. So the following pages are not for entertainment, not for relaxation, not for mystery or adventure, but they are for igniting a fire under your community. Most every community has their homeless population. Turning our backs on them or passing them by won't make them vanish off the face of the earth. So we sincerely have to deal with them in a way that will benefit them, which will, in turn, benefit the community.

This manual refers to the homeless as "Homeless" (participants in the program) and homeless (those who are not participants in the program). Also, keep in mind that the Homeless Project is not a program that gives money to the participants. That is the role of our state welfare agency.

So, to all those homeless persons that I passed by, I am truly sorry. But now I am trying to do something to make up for my actions.

La Verne Hughes, MEd
Counseling and Guidance

1

To Start With

Our Homeless Deserves Better!

The reason that I chose to refer to the homeless as "our homeless" is because they are. All of them have a mother and a father. They may even have brothers or sisters, aunts and uncles, grandparents, and so on. So they didn't arrive here on a UFO. They were born and raised right here on our planet Earth, which we all call home. They are a part of us all. They know it, and we should too.

But how and why did they become homeless? Well, if they are not of the categories "homeless by choice" and/or "scam artists," then their homeless status was forced upon them. Reasons for them becoming homeless can stem from running away from home to losing their home to a natural disaster.

And where are the relatives of these people? Busy with their own lives, trying to make ends meet, trying to keep *their* heads above water, financially speaking. Do they care about their homeless relative(s)? Do they even know that a relative of theirs is homeless? You'll have to ask them.

This manual will prove that it is not just up to the relatives of the homeless to care, but it is the responsibility of the community, as a whole, to care and aid them. An occasional meal, a temporary shelter, an armful of clothes won't take care of the problem. Could you live like that? I couldn't! Why should they?

Who Should Read This Manual?

I am hoping that college professors and students, businessmen, politicians, entertainers, neighbors, relatives, any- and everyone in your community will read this manual. And I hope all of you will understand what is being expressed in these pages. Community effort is a must.

So don't attempt the suggestions in this manual alone. You'll tire out before any good is done. Instead, share this book with others. Put your heads together as a united front. We have a growing epidemic on our hands, and it won't stop until we *all* do something about it together.

2

The Problem

More Is Needed Than What Is Currently Being Done

The problem of homelessness has existed since ancient times, and yet it still continues to exist. We cannot cure the epidemic of homelessness, but we can try to rectify, or alleviate, as much of the problem as we possibly can.

Noble efforts have been made and are still being made, but the problem has not gotten any better. Could it be that we are not utilizing every resource possible? Still, something more is needed. Let's see—we have soup kitchens, shelters, street comers, trash cans, back alleys, cardboard boxes big enough to sleep in. Did I leave out anything? Probably, but it apparently is still not enough.

The Buck Keeps Being Passed On

There are those of us who wait for someone else to do something about the problem. There are also those persons who say, "The homeless are nothing but drunks and drug addicts, so they don't deserve our help." I suppose that those families who lost their homes to natural disasters such as floods, tornadoes, etc., were boozin' it up or shootin' up at the time their homes were destroyed? Or maybe the teenager who ran away from an abusive home life was really just wanting the freedom to use drugs whenever he/she chose to? Or that mentally disabled person living in that cardboard box prefers living outdoors in the wintertime instead of being in a mental hospital. Maybe that's why the mental hospitals aren't getting the funds they need; so that their patients can have the comforts of home in a box.

How about that homeless person who is drunk in the alleyway, sitting in his urine? Surely he had enough money to buy a week's worth of food, but instead, he bought liquor. And why is that woman living in her car, and she even has a small child with her? So what if her husband physically and verbally abused her? She didn't have to work; she should have stayed in her warm home and taken the abuse. Her child would eventually grow up, and then he would understand why Daddy always beats on Mom. Surely all homeless people are homeless by choice—or are they? They're homeless now, so they'll just have to make the best of it—or can they?

Surely if they wanted to work, they could find a job somewhere—or can they? Would you hire a homeless person?

Waste Unchecked and Employment Unavailable

A major problem that I see is the wastefulness that goes on in our society. Food is wasted all the time in restaurants, cafeterias, bakeries, and other food establishments. To protect the consumer from food poisoning, harmful bacteria, and other germs, food is thrown out in large quantities. Yet a homeless person will eat from a garbage can just to survive yet another day. What is wrong with this picture?

Unemployment—another major problem. When a person fills out a job application, his name and address are required so that he can be contacted later. If you are homeless, what address will you write down? What are the chances of a homeless person living in a recognized shelter for the homeless or a cardboard box getting a job if his competition is you or your neighbor?

Oh yes, appearance is very important for landing a job. You are expected to display a clean-shaven, well-groomed, fresh-smelling, positive appearance when you go for that interview. You will also need transportation available to you. How many of the requirements listed above do you think the homeless person can acquire and then be able to beat out his competition for employment? Something to think about.

More Empathy for the Homeless Is Needed

It's time for us to become empathetic to the plight of the homeless and realize that they cannot do it alone. They need their community to stand up and take notice of them and their situation. They are crying for *help* but have lost hope in ever receiving the help that they truly need. Should we give up too? Not if it is in our power to do something.

The generosity of good-hearted persons has sometimes been taken advantage of. For instance, after having given money to a homeless person, you find out that the money was spent on booze or used for gambling. It is unfortunate, but there are going to be a few bad apples in the bunch. The Homeless Project should alleviate this problem, as shall be discussed.

3

What We Need to Do

Help from the Homeless Project

In order to give the homeless what they really need, several things are required. They are

1. the desire to help;
2. a plan of action;
3. a united effort from the community;
4. cooperation and a willingness to work together;
5. a common goal;
6. financial support through grants, donations from charities, etc.; and
7. services volunteered for certain aspects of the program.

The list goes on, but let's see how the Homeless Project can pull it all together.

The Homeless Project is not about eradicating homelessness off the face of the earth. The Homeless Project is a tool by which participating Homeless persons are empowered back to self-reliance and well-being. Once the Homeless participant is self-reliant again, he is then discharged from the program, a fortified individual, with pride in the community that gave him back his life.

The goal of the Homeless Project is *not* to give a free ride and handouts but to bring out of the Homeless person a self-sustained and confident individual, with few exceptions. Employment and one less homeless person are the outcomes. Wouldn't it be uplifting to know that if we should ever be *forced* into homelessness, the safety net of the Homeless Project is there, ready to catch us?

The Homeless Project is, in part, a task force that functions in the capacity of watchdog for the homeless. The task would be to set up committees with the responsibility of carrying out the plans and procedures of the various categories of homelessness. These categories are

1. the elderly,
2. the mentally disabled,
3. destitute families,
4. alcohol and drug addicts,
5. runaways,
6. the long-term unemployed, and
7. natural disaster victims.

Apparently, these categories exist because state aid was not available to them, jobs were not accessible, relatives were not in a position to help (or not aware), and the pursuit of life's goals had all but disappeared.

Each category has its own requirements, and yet some are similar.

1. The elderly
   a. Nursing home facility care
   b. Available transportation
   c. Relatives contacted
   d. State aid (welfare, Medicaid, Social Security, etc.)

2. The mentally disabled
   a. Mental health facility available
   b. Relatives contacted

3. The long-term unemployed, destitute family, and natural disaster victim
   a. State aid
   b. Employment
   c. Transportation
   d. Home address

4. Alcohol and drug addicts
   a. Medical treatment
   b. Counseling
   c. Close supervision to help with sobriety

    d. Employment after sobriety of a designated number of months

5. Runaways
    a. Counseling
    b. Wholesome recreation
    c. Relatives contacted
    d. Employment, if of an employable age

Your Community's Help Is Needed

What is needed from your community? A desire to help in any way requested by the Homeless Project Task Force. Such things as

1. businesses to offer employment and services;
2. treatment centers to provide medical care, with funding from Medicaid and other sources;
3. mental health facilities giving grants to accommodate homeless, mentally disabled patients;
4. state aid (welfare) to include Homeless Project participants in their services;
5. contractors to donate old houses, buildings, and trailers to the Homeless Project;
6. restaurants, cafeterias, and other eating establishments to donate their day-old, *refrigerated* food to the Homeless Project facilities that would be set up to receive it (this food would then be distributed to the various categories' kitchens or cafeterias);

7. relatives of the homeless to give moral and/or financial support;
8. transportation to the workplace would be made accessible (this, of course, would be at no charge to the participant until his first paycheck); and
9. an agency to donate funds for picture identification cards for each participant (these ID cards would not only identify the Homeless Project participant but would also identify the category of the participant).

These are just some of the requests that may be asked of the community.

What will be required of the participant?

1. To cooperate with the rules and regulations of the HP program
2. To accept the help given, with gratitude, for the *communities'* effort (recognizing that the community, as a whole, is offering these services)
3. To be a diligent employee
4. To help locate other homeless persons
5. To not panhandle (all necessities will be provided for through the HP program)

4

How to Give the Homeless What They Need

Homeless Participants Categorized

As mentioned previously, our homeless population is not made up of one group of homeless people, such as drunkards or drug addicts. Their population consists of a variety of groups and people (a nation within a nation). The major groups, or categories, being

1. the elderly,
2. the mentally disabled,
3. destitute families,
4. alcohol and drug addicts,
5. runaways,
6. long-term unemployed, and
7. natural disaster victims.

Quite naturally, we're talking about a wide range of age groups—from babies to old age. We're talking families, single people, or estranged spouses. Different races of people nationwide. A priority mission of the Homeless Project will be to locate all the homeless persons possible.

Besides using the help of homeless persons to locate others who are homeless, the HP will decide other means of accomplishing this huge task. But even *before* this can be done, shelter, food, clothing, jobs, transportation will need to already be available, accessible, and operating.

What Is Needed from the Community?

The biggest task for the HP will be to locate businesses that are willing and able to set aside job positions exclusively for the Homeless participants of the HP program. Needless to say, there will definitely need to be an added incentive for the business that will agree to this type of employment arrangement. But that incentive will be decided on between the task force and the business.

The next task will be shelter for the HP participants. This would include renovating old unused buildings and houses into dorms, rooms, and family units. Each category of the Homeless participants will have its own shelter facilities. Destitute families will not be mixed with alcohol and drug addicts, and so on. Each homeless category has its own specific needs, so each facility will be set up accordingly. Funding for this should come from charities and other voluntary donations. Plumbing, janitorial services, security, and maintenance are community obligations and should be treated as such. So monies from city taxes should also be funded to HP for these services to be acquired. The living facilities will *not* be given specific names that identify them as shelters for the homeless. This tends to add to the misgivings and stereotyping of the homeless by the community.

Food, another task, should be plentiful. But there is the matter of getting to it. The community's restaurants and other eating establishments that have good food to throw out will channel that food to HP living facilities. There will be committees set up just for this task of receiving food for the many living facilities.

Now the challenge—to contact relatives. No relative (that the Homeless participant wants notified) will be obligated to lend a helping hand. Yet those relatives will be told the circumstances of their Homeless relative, just in case they would like to help. Medical information and backgrounds about the Homeless relative will be asked of the relative contacted. (Records will be kept on the Homeless participants for a period of time.) Some relatives may choose to take over the responsibilities of their Homeless relative, but depending on the category, the HP will need to be in agreement with this arrangement. The goal of HP is to see that all participants will eventually become one with society again. If the contacted relative can accomplish this, the HP will more than likely agree to the arrangement.

Of course, all Homeless participants will be eligible for food stamps, Medicaid, Social Security, etc., but they will be under the same restrictions and obligations as other welfare recipients. They will also be eligible for Section 8 and other city housing arrangements, depending on the participants' category.

The Homeless participants who will have a more difficult time becoming eligible for state aid will be the alcohol and drug addicts. These will be responsible for staying alcohol- and drug-free for a certain length of time. That will also be necessary for them to be eligible for employment. They will live under a strict regimen and receive clinical attention. Any who do not cooperate will be expelled from the program. Panhandling, begging, etc., will not be tolerated. With the HP in operation, begging and scrounging for food will not be necessary.

Funding will also be channeled into the mental health facilities. The mentally disabled homeless persons are an endangerment to themselves and others. They should be located and returned to the appropriate mental health facility. After being cleared for release by an authorized mental health personnel, they will then be eligible to live in an HP living facility until they can live independently.

In order to be registered with the Homeless Project, a picture ID card will be issued. These cards will not only identify the person and that this person is an HP participant but also the category that this Homeless person is affiliated with. (This registration should also help create a more accurate national census report.)

Help That Each Category Needs

Each category, of course, requires help that will differ slightly from the others. For this reason, each category will require a different and separate committee to provide what is needed.

The Elderly

Besides relatives being contacted, the elderly will require nursing facility care as well as independent living quarters. Volunteer nursing staff would be available to monitor those elderly who are living independently in an HP living facility. Health will determine who is transferred to either the nursing care facility or an HP living facility. When a social security or other type of income has been established, the independent living participants will be eligible for Section 8, a housing project facility for the elderly, or other community living arrangement. Their health, living conditions, and general well-being will be closely monitored by HP. Transportation will be provided by a community transit system. Funding for this will be provided through HP's channels.

The Mentally Disabled

All mentally disabled participants and those suspected as such will be evaluated by a mental health professional. The evaluation will be discussed professionally with the HP committee for the mentally disabled. The participant will then be admitted into a mental health facility or an HP living facility. HP living facilities for the mentally disabled are closely monitored and will have a mental health staff member present at all times. The goal of the HP living facility is to provide shelter for the participant until they have proven their self-reliance. Self-reliance not only includes being able to care for themselves but being able to participate in the HP job program. Section 8 and other city and state programs would also be available to those living in an HP living facility.

Relatives would need to be contacted for the benefit of receiving vital health information about the participant. The relative would also be made aware of the living arrangements provided for the participant.

Destitute Families and Natural Disaster Victims

The Red Cross is a major source of help for families who are victims of natural disasters, fires, and other misfortunes that can come up on any one of us. The HP is the "sustainer" after the Red Cross has fulfilled its mission. The HP allows the participants' families the time they need in order to get back on their feet again. This amount of time will vary from family to family. A temporary home until a more permanent home is acquired is sometimes all that is needed. Relatives may need to be contacted, employers contacted, insurance agents contacted; any number of people or agencies may need to be contacted. This would be done in the comfort of an HP living facility.

Transportation to jobs, insurance agents, etc., would be provided for through the transit system. State aid would also be available if necessary.

Alcohol and Drug Addicts

This category will pose a major challenge. Medical treatment and clinical assistance for sobriety will be a must. Group counseling, wholesome recreation, and close supervision will also be a must. The biggest challenge, though, will be the participants' *willingness* to cooperate with the program. For instance, panhandling will be forbidden. Anyone found panhandling will be held accountable. With all the provisions being supplied for by the HP, there would be no need for panhandling. The police department will be working closely with this category's committee to help control these occurrences.

The HP living facilities for this category will have guards on staff and on the premises at all times. The living facility is to be a safe haven for *all* participants. Sobriety will be a goal pushed by the committee for all participants. As to how this will be handled, medical as well as committee members will decide the format for this.

For those participants who remain sober for a certain length of time, employment will be the next goal. This is all pointing toward a sober and successful transition back into society as an independent and selfreliant individual. State aid would also be available to the participant at this time.

Runaways

Runaways are looking for a safe haven, generally speaking. With a safe haven comes people whom the runaway can *trust*. To locate runaways, word of mouth will probably be the main way to go.

They will not be forced to be an HP participant (no participant is forced), but they will be encouraged to become HP participants.

The only relatives contacted, if any, will be decided upon by the runaway. As to whether foster care or another state agency would be contacted will be based on the runaway's age. If a runaway is of an employable age, then employment will be a priority. Counselors will be available and on staff at the living facility. Older and mature individuals will live in the living facility (volunteers) as a source of comfort and stability for the participant. Transportation and wholesome recreation will be available, as with the other categories.

All categories deserve help and understanding from the community, but all participants are requiring the opportunity to get back on their feet again and be a part of society in a *real* sense. Not pity, but respect and opportunity.

In the meantime, their needs still have to be met on a daily basis. The Homeless Project is a vital and urgent channel for bringing lives of homeless persons back into mainstream society.

5

Sources of Help

Recycle Discarded Goods

The major sources to provide the necessary provisions, such as food, clothing, and other household items, will be the local food establishments, clothing stores, department stores, and any other establishment that discards usable products. There should be no charge from these establishments to HP because these items were being discarded anyway. HP would be responsible for pickup and delivery of all items acquired.

As mentioned before, old buildings, old apartments, and old houses could be donated to HP for living facilities and housing units. Renovation of these facilities would be a community effort of sorts. Volunteers, donations, and any other constructional help would be needed. Shelters that are already in existence should become one with the HP program as a joint effort. So, this would include organizations such as the Salvation Army. None should have to do it alone. For maintenance and custodial services of these living facilities, certain HP participants would be trained in those capacities. More than likely, alcohol and drug addicts, who are working on their sobriety, would be used as volunteers. This would also be job experience that could be used on their job résumé or application when they have reached the point of eligibility for regular employment.

Something else that is very vital to the success of the program is this—we *need* to apportion state and city funds back into our mental health institutes.

I would like you to pause.

Take a *deep* breath. Hold it. Now, let it out *slowly*. This is no time to get our feathers ruffled because of the possibility of more taxes being asked for. Remember, this is a community effort and should be a statewide, if not nationwide, effort on our part. Funding to mental health institutions can also come from businesses, individuals, charities, as well as research funds. So, by doing this, a major portion of the homeless problem will be brought under control.

How to Reach Those Sources of Help

Certain steps have to be taken to get the Homeless Project off the ground. Because this project will be monumental, to say the least, it will first need to be looked at from certain aspects, such as economical, social, and community development. Universities and colleges are in a very good position to do this because of the fresh ideas and open-mindedness of their students.

After a thorough study of what would be involved (by the different field-of-study departments), a joint departmental study would be done to pull all ideas and reports together. If the prospects look promising, then the mayor of the city/ community would be notified and met with for a discussion of the report. If the mayor is in agreement, then a task force would be set up and committees formed for starting the Homeless Project.

6

A Worthwhile Outcome

Take the First Step

Will your community be able to say, "Yes, we cared, and we also chose to do something about our community's homeless problem"? It is a matter of choice. No one is forcing your community to do this. But what if *your* circumstances change for the worse? Would you prefer living in a box, desperate for just a few snatches of food, or would you prefer comforts like home? Your choice!

It takes time to bring about the smooth operation of a program like the Homeless Project. Maybe you have the time, but while you sit and ponder on whether to take the first step or not, another homeless person is dying from the community's neglect. It could even be a relative of yours.

On the other hand, if you do decide that you will do something, you will gain a sense of purpose and peace of mind as you take the first step. That first step, of course, is to take this manual to your community's mayor. The next step is his/hers. You have thus opened the way for our homeless to get the help they deserve.

A Major Drop in the Number of Homeless Persons

The startling outcome for the community with an HP program will be a *drop* in the numbers of people without a place to live, without food to eat regularly, without proper medical care, without enough clothing, and without a sense of belongingness. For those homeless persons who choose not to be a part of the HP program—their numbers will be very small—their struggle will continue to be monumental. It will also become disgraceful not to be a part of the HP program and remain an added burden.

Other Communities to Follow Your Example

After your community has accomplished the tremendous task of being able to rectify your community's homeless problem, and after your community has made the national news, then other communities will follow your example. Your community will become a leader, a history maker, as well as an outstanding model for other communities to follow—a strong community.

Strong communities make for a stronger nation.

America, the land of opportunity, will truly be the land of opportunity for *all* its citizens. America is looked to as a leader by many countries. Let's take the lead in giving our homeless the help they deserve.

The HomelessProject Corporation

A Brief Overview of the Staff Positions

I. Founder and program auditor (a quality control position)

    A. Will work closely with the coordinator and program planner

    B. Will oversee the Field Representative Department.

    C. Will act as a complaint office

        1. Complaints from participants

        2. Complaints from staff members

        3. Complaints from other interested persons

    D. Will hold meetings to discuss

        1. changes needed,

        2. complaints and what to do about them, and

        3. updates on progress made as to quality, or lack of quality, by the corporation.

E. Will have authority to appoint or dismiss salaried staff members

F. Will audit the overall operation of the corporation, from the participant to the staff member

G. Will assist with problem solving

II. Coordinator

A. Will implement and authorize services of the corporation

B. Will have authority to appoint or dismiss staff members with the permission of the founder

C. Will oversee the departments of the program planner, office for volunteers, fundraising, treasurer, personnel, and program auditor (after the founder has appointed another to the position of program auditor)

D. Will hold meetings to discuss issues that arise

III. Program planner

A. Will organize and develop strategies for the corporation

B. Will work closely with the program auditor, Field Representative Department, Fundraising Department, and treasurer

C. Will receive reports from the Needs Department

D. Will receive requests and concerns from the Categories Department

IV. Office of Volunteers

    A. Will hire the corporation's volunteers

    B. Will assign the volunteers where needed

    C. Will work closely with the program planner

    D. Will receive requests for volunteers from the Needs Department and assign volunteers accordingly

Volunteers will be candidates for hire on a paid capacity.

V. Fundraising Department

    A. Will assess the financial needs of the corporation as they arise

    B. Will work closely with the program planner and treasurer

    C. Will devise fundraising strategies (strategies will require the approval of the coordinator before they are implemented)

VI. Treasurer

    A. Will be responsible for budgets and expenditures

    B. Will work closely with the Personnel and Fundraising Departments

    C. Will work closely with outside accountant

    D. Will do bookkeeping and other accounting duties

    E. Will do internal economy and efficiency audits (making sure that the corporation has complied fully with the laws and regulations governing not-for-profit organizations; these reports will be forwarded to the coordinator, program planner, and the program auditor)

F. Will be responsible for issuing all checks (salary, program, etc.)

VII. Personnel

A. Will be authorized to hire and fire hourly employees, based on supervisor's recommendations

B. Will work closely with the treasurer in regard to salary and hourly wages

C. Will be responsible for arranging and providing tours for touring visitors

VIII. Assessment clerk

A. Will receive and gather data on incoming participants

B. Will determine which category the participant will be assigned to

C. Will work closely with the Categories Department

IX. Field Representative Department

A. Will be responsible for developing a Homeless Project service in other *large* communities

B. Will work closely with the program planner and the program auditor

C. Will also be available for giving tours
D. Will set up a website online for other communities in need of setting up a Homeless Project service
E. Will hold seminars upon request
F. Will provide the spokesperson for the corporation

Travel will be a large part of this position.

Needs Department

I. Outreach

A. Will contact relatives of participants, with the participants' permission
B. Will provide a network for locating homeless persons

1. Participants who know other homeless persons
2. Red Cross, etc. (natural disaster victims, evictions, etc.)
3. Other agencies that are contacted by homeless persons
4. A hotline (1-800-?) for anyone—homeless persons as well as persons who suspect that someone is homeless—to contact the corporation

C. Will locate homeless persons from surrounding communities

II. Housing and Land Development

    A. Will contact realtors and land developers for suitable housing and land (trailers, duplexes, lots for sale, etc.)

    B. Will attend land and property auctions

    C. Will establish housing units as per the needs of Categories

III. Food, Clothing, Furnishings, etc.

    A. Will be responsible for locating sources of food, etc. (restaurants, department stores, food banks, etc.)

    B. Will be responsible for pickup and delivery of food, clothing, etc.

        1. This department will have vehicles for the purpose of pickup and delivery.

        2. Acquiring vehicles will be done through

            a. the donation of vehicles,

            b. automobile and truck auctions, and

            c. the purchase of repossessed vehicles.

    C. Will arrange with department stores and furniture stores to collect damaged and discarded goods before they are set out for trash pickup

    D. Will work closely with Categories to assess their needs

All foods and other items will be for the use of each category.

IV. Transportation

    A. Will be responsible for providing transportation for the participants

    B. Will request assistance from the OATS bus service to provide transportation for category Elderly

V. Medical and Family Contact

    A. Will work closely with Categories in assessing medical needs of each participant

    B. Will contact family members of participants concerning their medical history

    C. Will work closely with cooperating hospital(s) and medical staff in seeing that the participants' needs are met (Medicaid, Medicare, and other family insurances should be utilized when medical payments are required)

VI. Job Finder

    A. Will be responsible for locating businesses willing to hire participants

    B. Will work closely with Categories

    C. Will make assessments of the participants' job qualifications and abilities

D. Will provide supervision for participants who do custodial and maintenance work as well as other duties performed for the corporation (this experience will be added to the participant's job history)

Categories Department

Categories I through

VII. Heads of these categories

A. Will be responsible for assessing the specific needs of their particular category
B. Will work closely with the Needs Department
C. Will receive their participants from the assessment clerk's recommendations
D. Will report their category's needs to the appropriate departments such as the Needs Department, program planner, Office of Volunteers, etc.

Each category will have access to the resources provided by the Needs Department.

Strategies

1. Will set up in an already existing building
2. Will acquire more staff as the corporation grows
3. Will use the spokesperson (field representative) for radio and television interviews as well as newspaper write-ups, etc.

4. Will need to find a way to channel funding into the mental health hospital(s) for the benefit of our mentally disabled participants

The goal of the corporation is to become a nationwide organization. The existing social and human services and agencies (e.g., Salvation Army, Advent, OATS bus service, Red Cross, etc.) will all extend their services to the corporation.

Money Sources to Consider

1. HUD Continuum of Care
2. Government grants
3. Fundraisers
4. Donations from organizations, businesses, and private individuals
5. Resources already acquired (take an inventory)
6. Gifts of charity
7. Federated funders (banks and other financial institutions)
8. Foundations
9. Fees from communities requesting our services in setting up a Homeless Project service for their community
10. Proceeds from the sale of the book *Our Homeless Deserves Better!* of which a percentage would be channeled to the Homeless Project Corporation

CPSIA information can be obtained at www.ICGtesting.com
Printed in the USA
LVOW10s0354140716

495511LV00010B/109/P

9 781682 373262